CONTENTS

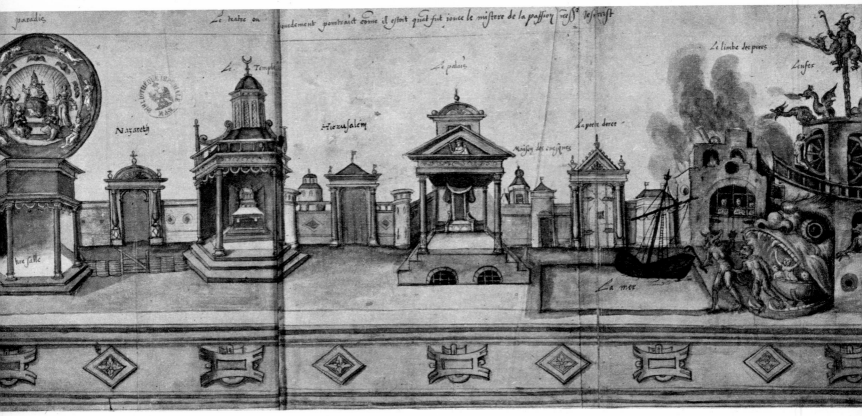

DESIGNER
Germano Facetti

EDITOR
David Lambert

ART
Kempster and Evans
Bernard Myers
Peter Sullivan

Printed in Great Britain by L. T. A. Robinson Ltd., London

J.B.Priestley

The Wonderful World of the
Theatre

© 1959, Rathbone Books Limited Library of Congress Card Catalog No. 59-10089
GARDEN CITY BOOKS   **GARDEN CITY**   **NEW YORK**

Faun costume for 'Fête de Bacchus' and other 18th-century operas

Theatre assumes all shapes, means all things to all people: entertainment to a small court audience amused by the French 'faun's' graceful gestures; livelihood to an entire Red Indian tribe depending on this magic dance for good hunting and a food-supply.

What is Theatre?

This book is about the Theatre, from the earliest times to the present day. We shall be taking a look at all manner of actual theatres, existing at many different places. But all these belong to – are varying expressions of – the essential Theatre: the one we print with a capital letter.

Before we follow the history of the Theatre through so many centuries, we ought to try to understand what the Theatre is all about, why it has lasted so long, what it means to us. We know that it offers amusement and pleasure, but then so do lots of other things. Is there something special

to itself that it offers us? Clearly there is, otherwise the Theatre would not have gone on so long and in so many different places. But what is it that is special about the Theatre?

True, when we see a play we see it with a number of other people; we form part of an audience. This is important, because we behave differently when we are part of an audience. If the play is funny, we laugh a great deal more than we should if we were by ourselves. If it is pathetic, we are more deeply moved just because a lot of other people are being moved too. And notice this, we cannot enjoy

Theatre thrives with and without human actors: is present in a Shakespeare play and in a puppet-show – itself a Theatre assuming many shapes throughout the world, from the familiar Punch-and-Judy of the West to Eastern Java's strangely-painted marionettes.

Puppet-masters provide the actors' voices for their marionettes; but Theatre also thrives on words unspoken: is present in the poetry of Shakespeare but also in the age-old art of silent mime. Pictured above is Marcel Marceau, master-artist of modern mime.

the play at all unless it is having the same effect upon us as it is having upon all the other members of the audience around us.

We have to share the feelings of a great many other people to enjoy a play properly, and this in itself is a good thing, particularly these days, when too many people, usually living in large cities, feel cut off and separate and lonely. To enjoy the Theatre we have to *join in* ; and we feel better after it in the same way (though to a lesser degree) that we feel better after attending some religious service or great public meeting.

Now all this business of being part of an audience, which is essential to the Theatre, is very important. But it still leaves unexplained what the Theatre has to offer its spectators that other public gatherings and other forms of amusement cannot offer them. Is there some kind of experience that we enjoy at a play and nowhere else? And if there is – then what is it? This is a question easy to ask, but, as we know from the work of dramatic critics and theorists at many different times who have asked themselves the same question, very difficult to answer adequately. Now we will try.

Disguised beneath white-painted faces, smart harlequin costumes, or long-haired, bowler-hatted, baggy-trousered and frowzy, modern circus-clowns amuse ringside millions with their drollness of wit or more often with horseplay, buffoonery, wild comic antics.

The cap-and-bells and 'weapon' – an inflated pig's bladder – were the costume of a court jester – a clown 600 years ago. Theatrical conventions change but never disappear; none is more striking than the 'uniforms' identifying comedians from the past and present.

A theatrical production consists of a number of players acting imaginary characters. Here are two quite different elements – the real actors, the imaginary characters. We have to accept them both; and this is where theorists of dramatic art have gone wrong, for they have generally accepted one to the exclusion of the other. And this simply will not work as the following reasons show.

If we say we go to the play only to follow the fortunes of the imaginary characters then we have to assume, what certainly is not true, that we do not know we are in a playhouse, looking at and listening to actors.

If we go to the other extreme, as some critics have done, and say we go to the play for the acting, then what becomes of the play itself, the imaginary life of its characters? Why should these unreal people and what happens to them have any interest for us, when we know it is all make-believe, just so many actors performing?

Nearly all theorists of the drama have been baffled by this dilemma, simply because they have assumed that the experience offered us by the Theatre must be based on either the imaginary life of the play or on the reality of the performance. And clearly it cannot be. Both elements must contribute to the experience, which is complex, involving two different levels of the mind. One level is accepting the imaginary life of the play and its characters. The other level is concerned with the actual presentation of the play, with the theatre, stage, actors, scenery, lighting and effects.

A very young child generally cannot accept the experience, assumes that what is happening on the stage is real, and is either frightened or bored, wanting to run up and down the aisle to play. A year or two later, the same child may be enchanted, eagerly following the fortunes of the characters and yet at the same time being tremendously conscious of sitting snugly in the theatre with Mummy or Daddy. It is this eager responsiveness on both levels that makes children such a splendid audience. Adults who have completely forgotten their childhood, who have allowed all wonder and imagination to wither away, who are really incapable of making this double response, are never keen playgoers and usually dislike the Theatre.

This, then, is dramatic experience; the result of an appeal to two different levels of the mind and of a corresponding response on both levels. And as on one level we are fully conscious of being in a theatre, watching and listening to actors, it follows that on this level we accept whatever convention of theatrical writing, production and acting may be in vogue; that all drama depends upon some convention – a generally accepted pretense that something is something else. There are many different kinds of convention as we shall see; but all of them have and always have had one central purpose – to offer audiences that unique type of experience which we can call dramatic experience. It is to provide this that the Theatre exists.

A Javanese actor's conventional mask. Eastern performers of dramas and dance-dramas don such masks, painted with the faces of the characters they represent. Eastern audiences know an actor plays a sad or happy role because his mask forever frowns or smiles.

Sir Alec Guinness making-up. Greasepaint, not masks, is Western Theatre's convention for making actors old or young, happy or sad. But in East and West those audiences enjoy drama most who are watching both characters and the actors who portray them.

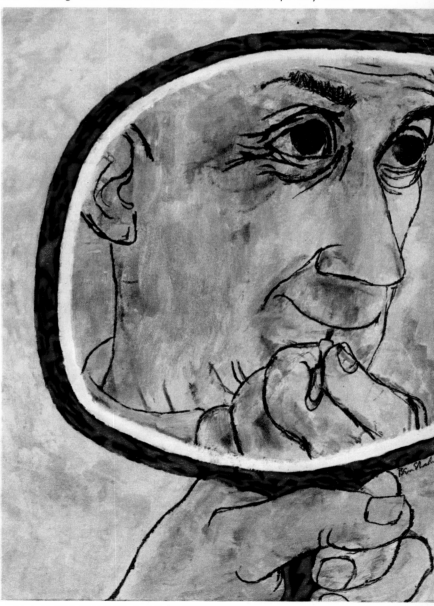

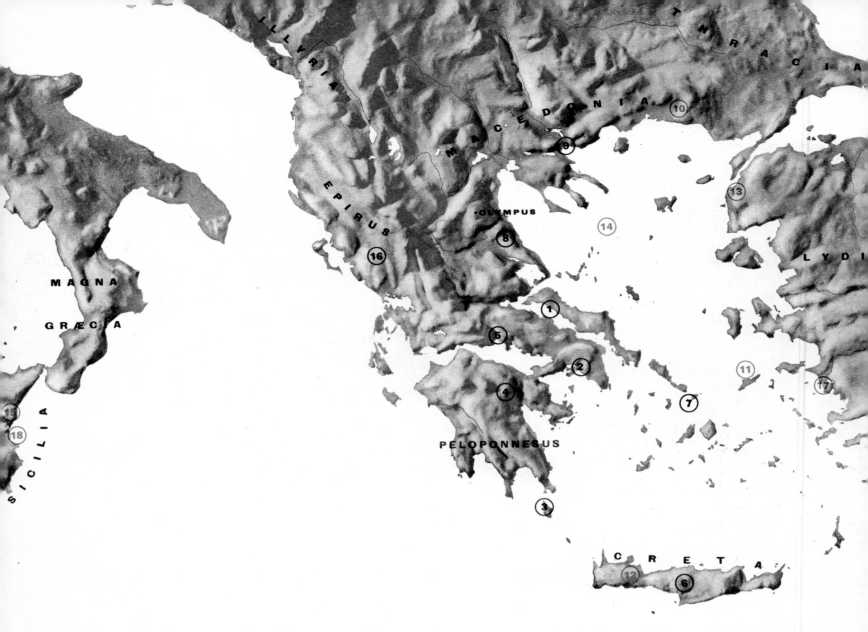

The ancient Greek world, thickly sown with scenes of legendary deeds by gods and heroes – themes of the first plays. Black numbers refer to gods, red, to mortals: (1) Poseidon's undersea palace; (2) Athene, patron of Athens; (3) Aphrodite, born of the sea's foam; (4) Hermes; (5) Apollo; (6) Zeus, born on Cretan Mt. Ida; (7) Artemis; (8) Centaurs; (9) Dionysus; (10) Orpheus; (11) Icarus falls after flying too near the sun; (12) Heracles defeats the Cretan bull; (13) Helen and Paris at Troy; (14) Argonauts sail to Lemnos; (15) Odysseus in Sicily; (16) Oracular Dove of Dodona; (17) Miletus kills a giant; (18) Cyclops. Olympus: seat of gods

Magic and Tragedy

Men must have been performing long before history began. Primitive men believed in what we now call 'sympathetic magic' – the idea that if you act something you can make it happen. A hunting tribe running short of meat might decide to act the discovery and killing of a deer. If so, somebody had to pretend to be the deer, and others pretend to be the successful hunters. In its own fashion, this is as much a performance as a production of *Hamlet*.

As religions developed, the public rites connected with them involved some elements of production, acting, performance. Long before Athens became a city-state and the home of a magnificent civilisation, the Greeks had made use of choral hymns and dances in their worship; and during seasonal fertility rites had enjoyed revels and masquerades in which the performers pretended to be birds and other animals. It is generally held that we can discover in hymns and dances the origin of Greek Tragedy, and in revels and masquerades the origin of Greek Comedy.

Although theatres grew up everywhere in Greece, it is to Athens at its height during the fifth century B.C. that we owe the complete development of the Theatre and one of the greatest dramatic styles the world has known. It was a completely communal art: performed not for private amusement but at great public festivals, where the most important dramatic poets competed for civic prizes.

Although this classical Greek drama was true drama, its general style and atmosphere might suggest to us a kind of solemn opera rather than a play. Both tragedy and comedy were originally formal and conventional, following strict rules broken later by dramatists of genius. Both included music and dancing. Both employed a Chorus which, in tragedy, spoke with the voice of the community, expressing common points of view.

A legend relates how the god Dionysus (inventor of wine), when attacked by pirates, made a magic vine climb the mast before turning his terrified foes into dolphins.

Tragic dramatists did not invent stories and characters. Their dramas were based on myths and legends familiar to everybody. Suspense and surprise were absent from this Theatre, but in terms of high poetic tragedy this was an advantage. The poets could concentrate upon giving their own interpretation of familiar stories. Since everybody knew what must happen, the poets could make use of dramatic irony; could show a proud man who thinks himself master of his fate, moving inevitably to the doom which the audience knows awaits him.

11

A Dionysiac procession on a Greek vase which may recall the frenzied drama of an actual performance of ritual song and dance

Dionysus, god of the vine. To him were dedicated festive rites at seed-time and harvest when worshippers danced and sang.

Bare hillsides were the first Greek theatres; spectators standing on their slopes watched the chorus performing the ritual of songs and dances on the round orchestra (a 'dancing place') below.

Ritual dance became drama which spectators watched from terraced seats made of wood, later of stone. Behind the orchestra a simple building rose whence actors appeared, to play their parts.

In Roman times, the auditorium became an artificial 'hill' raised on vaults. Stone scene-buildings cut into half the orchestra; most acting was now on stages which were raised between the two.

Most beautiful and best-preserved of Greek theatres is Epidaurus, begun in the 4th century B.C. Today it attracts tourists of all nations with new performances of the world's most ancient drama.

Built in a sunny climate, a Greek theatre (the word meant 'seeing place') stood open to the sky. In spite of its immense auditorium —
Epidaurus could seat 12,000 — an actor's words were clearly heard from the farthest seats. Audiences saw dramas ('things done' or 'performed') which included tragedy (perhaps from 'goatsong' since goats were sacrificed at rites) and comedy (from the Greek for 'revel').

Unlike later dramas, which could be printed and so endlessly duplicated, ancient Greek dramas only existed as fragile manuscripts. Far more of them have disappeared than have survived. But the surviving dramas, coming to us almost miraculously after centuries of war, invasion, revolution, show us what a height Greek tragedy suddenly achieved. Tradition has it that the poet Thespis of Athens first used an actor as well as a chorus-leader, and this has brought him his own immortality for whatever concerns acting has since been called by the name 'Thespian'.

The first of the three great Greek tragic masters, Aeschylus (525–456 B.C.), introduced a second actor, which really made drama as we understand it possible. He was also celebrated for his startling effects, such as the tremendous entrance of Agamemnon in a chariot.

The second of these great tragic poets, Sophocles (c.496–406 B.C.), was less of an innovator, but he introduced a third actor, made less use of the chorus, and is said to have been the first dramatist to insist upon painted scenery.

The third, Euripides (c.484–406 B.C.), made still less use of the chorus but greatly increased the number of characters in his plays. (There are as many as eleven in the *Phoenician Women*.)

Greek scholars down the centuries have varied considerably in their estimates of Aeschylus, Sophocles and Euripides according to their own temperaments and outlook. Here we must look at them very broadly from the standpoint of world Theatre. Aeschylus was the grand originator, the first great dramatist known to us; and considered simply as a tragic poet, must be held to be the greatest. His wonderful trilogy – a group of three plays – the *Oresteia*, which shows how one crime breeds another in the doomed family of Atreus until at last civic justice (civilisation) is achieved, is a towering masterpiece of dramatic force and lofty imagination.

Regarded simply as a dramatist, Sophocles is the greatest of the three. Of all these tragedies, his *Oedipus Rex* has been played most frequently in our own Theatre. It is a short play: a marvel of tense, terse writing, and terrible dramatic irony, as within two hours the ill-fated Oedipus makes one appalling discovery after another about himself, and is changed from a king to an outcast.

Greek vase depicts Prometheus punished by Zeus for bringing man-kind fire – a myth retold in Aeschylus' play 'Prometheus Bound'.

Opinions differ widely about Euripides. Admirers of Sophocles and Aeschylus think him inferior and see in his work the ruin of the classical tradition. Other critics put him first because he is better at describing individual people, gives more scope for acting, is more romantic in feeling, altogether less bound by classical rules and more like a modern writer. Indeed it is hard to believe Euripides was a contemporary of Sophocles. The main idea in the older and more strictly classical Greek plays is the relation between man and the powers of the universe. In the plays of Euripides this is being replaced by the relation between one man and another, and by the idea, familiar in modern drama, that character shapes destiny.

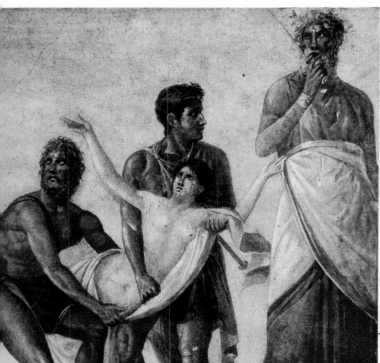

(Left) Graeco-Roman fresco showing scene from the ancient legend of Iphigenia, sacrificed by her own father to appease an angry goddess – the theme for Euripides' play 'Iphigenia in Aulis'.

2,000 years of classic drama: a modern production of 17th-century play, based on Roman drama, in Greek theatre at Taormina, Sicily.

Actors dressing in a 'green room', perhaps 2,000 years ago. This mosaic made in Italian Pompeii when still a Greek settlement, reminds us that Greece inspired Rome's drama as well as other arts.

Aristophanes (c.448–380B.C.): most famous author of 'Old Comedy'

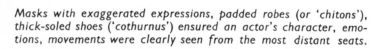

Masks with exaggerated expressions, padded robes (or 'chitons'), thick-soled shoes ('cothurnus') ensured an actor's character, emotions, movements were clearly seen from the most distant seats.

Greek comedy took longer to develop than Greek tragedy and had no place in civic festivals for half a century. This is easy to understand. The Old Comedy – quite different from the later New Comedy – combined so many elements, choral, miming, dialogue, clowning, that only a writer of genius could fuse them successfully into drama worth a place beside the work of the tragic poets.

This genius was Aristophanes, and though his plays are rarely produced today, he must be included in any list of the world's great comic writers. His plays are too fantastic, too much 'of their time' to have had much direct dramatic influence, but many later comic writers, especially between 1500–1750, studied his work to their advantage, borrowing and adapting many of his droll ideas. He often chose a theme enabling him to use a 'masquerade' chorus as in his *Wasps, Birds, Frogs*; and introduced topical allusions and jokes, with savage, though very funny, skits on well-known characters like Euripides and Socrates.

The nearest thing we have to the Aristophanic Old Comedy is the satirical show, filled with rude remarks about people known to the audience, put together by students as an end-of-term 'rag'.

In his later plays, sometimes called Middle Comedy, Aristophanes is less fantastic and savage, cuts down the part played by the chorus to make room for more plot and acting. The contemporary interest of the drama may be judged by the fact that in *The Frogs*, Aeschylus and Euripides are competing in Hades for the privilege of returning to Athens to revive the declining art of tragedy.

The New Comedy was at its height about a hundred years later. Unfortunately only fragments of its plays survive. There is however enough of Menander, its most important dramatist, to show us what kind of drama it was. Unlike the Old Comedy – fantastic, topical, local – the New Comedy is not peculiar to a time and place, reduces the chorus to a little singing and dancing between the scenes or acts, and deals with situations and types of character that were to make their appearance over and over again, starting with the Roman dramas of Plautus and Terence. Menander and his fellow dramatists created the comedy of intrigue, character, manners that became popular in the seventeenth and eighteenth centuries and has persisted, with some changes of style, right down to the present day.

The rich and tyrannical old man, the wild young man who can be tamed by the right girl, the devoted nuisance of a servant – these and other familiar types were making their first appearance on the stage 2,250 years ago in Athens. The 'new comedy' advertised to appear next week, with its elegant witty dialogue, its impudent intrigues, its amusing clash of characters, descends directly down the ages from this New Comedy of ancient Greece.

Patterned in Roman mosaic, this white-faced mask of tragedy and red-faced mask of comedy follow already ancient stage traditions.

Beneath such grotesque masks and padded bellies lurked the comedians of 2,000 years ago.

17

A scene from an ancient comedy. Old men, youth and servant – Greek types of comic character – later gained popularity in many lands.

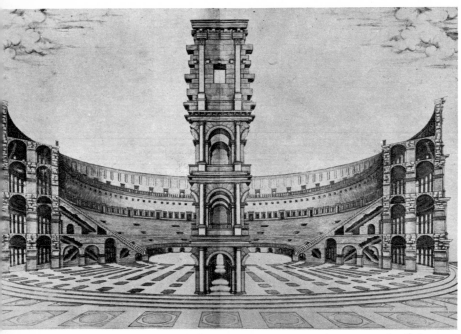

A tribute to Rome's engineers in stone and concrete, the Colosseum (a two-theatres-in-one amphitheatre) held 50,000 spectators. (Below) 'Tickets' twenty centuries old prove classic theatre-goers and circus-spectators paid for their seats much as we do today.

(Above) ? Lucius Annaeus Seneca (4 B.C.-65 A.D.). Played little in his time, bloodthirsty Senecan tragedies delighted Shakespeare's day. (Below) Publius Terentius Afer (c.195-159B.C.). Once a slave, Terence lived to become the best-known comic dramatist of his age.

The Romans built magnificent theatres. Unlike the Greeks who used only natural hill-sites, they could raise their theatres and amphitheatres anywhere because of their skill in erecting vaults which would support rising tiers of seats and galleries.

During the Republic, Roman imitations of the New Comedy of Athens held the stage for many years, and gave Terence and Plautus their reputations. But under the Empire the Theatre declined very sharply. Men of letters like Seneca amused themselves writing plays, but plays which they intended to be read and not performed.

The Roman Theatre was now no place for a dignified man of letters. It was simply part of the local amusements, on no higher level than wrestling, combats between gladiators and wild-animal shows. Actors, though often highly-paid popular figures, were not reputable citizens. Meaningless spectacles, scenes of violence, buffoonery and obscenity found their way into these shows to amuse the jaded aristocrats and Roman mobs.

When Christianity spread so widely, making many enthusiastic converts, the Theatre was merely an obscene shadow of itself. Christians were strictly forbidden to attend it – and when finally the Church had the necessary power, it excommunicated the actors and began closing the theatres. Traces of this first bad relationship between Christianity and the Theatre lingered on. Millions of people to this day imagine that the Theatre, which was of course actually religious in its roots, is profoundly irreligious.

But one development of this decadent Roman Theatre is worth mentioning. Throughout the provinces there were wandering troupes, generally consisting of slaves owned by the master of the troupe, who would set up their little platforms and curtains and play a number of short scenes, sometimes in mime or dumb show (especially when the players could not speak the local language), sometimes improvising rough dialogue and topical jokes. The players were often acrobats, tumblers, dancers, as well as actors of a sort.

After the theatres were closed, little troupes of players still went on their travels; and it is more than likely that some never stopped performing throughout the Dark Ages when the Theatre was forgotten. After a thousand years or so, what had once been the magnificent Attic drama, with its civic festivals, tragedies and comedies that are

Rome's greatest spectacle: the Colosseum flooded for a 'sea-fight'

among the notable achievements of the human mind, the Theatre had dwindled to a few carts and platforms and humble troupes of clowns and acrobats. But something was kept alive, however degraded its outer appearance. There were still performers and audiences. Men still made other men stare and laugh and wonder by some skill, however rudimentary, in the ancient art of acting.

Incidents in the life of Christ inspired the medieval Mystery plays which gave rebirth to the Theatre. Here, depicted by medieval artists, are (left) Christ's Presentation at the Temple, (above) Christ leaving the Praetorium, (below) Christ on the Way to Calvary.

Mystery and Macbeth

Throughout western Europe during the later Middle Ages the drama slowly came to life again, at first by way of the Church. In the cathedrals and larger churches it became customary at Easter and Christmas to include in the special services a few brief scenes, played by priests, illustrating the birth and death of Jesus. These drew such crowds that more elaborate versions of them began to be played outside, generally on and around the steps.

Finally the Church refused to allow priests to take part in these outside performances, which were taken over by laymen. These lay performers might belong to special companies organised for the purpose, as in France, or, as in England, to the trade guilds, which were responsible for producing various Mystery plays (after *ministerium:* service) at festival times.

Both the plays, though still crude when considered as drama, and their staging became more and more elaborate. In southern Europe old Roman theatres were used, wooden seats were built, rough-and-ready stage machinery was contrived, and the fires and torments of Hell awaiting the wicked personages of the drama were suggested by various stage effects. In England the guilds staged productions in a different way, important because it led to the Elizabethan theatre – the setting for Shakespeare's plays. English guilds used great wagons on which small wooden sets were built; these wagons served both as backgrounds and upper stages, with the ground in front as the lower stage. Their Mysteries too were less solemn, more popular in style than those of France, and characters like the Devil and Herod were often turned into comics.

Following the Mystery came the Morality, religious in feeling but dramatising good and bad qualities and their effect upon ordinary men. The most famous Morality, which is still often played both in theatres and out of doors, was *Everyman*.

We leave the Middle Ages for the Renaissance, with its new sense of discovery, freedom and adventure, its passionate interest in the classical life and literature of ancient Greece and Rome, its growing wealth and cities with their opulent way of life. Italy, filled with artists and scholars, ruled by cultured princes and dukes, led western Europe on the way towards our secular modern Theatre.

Mystery and Miracle ('lives of the saints') plays saw the beginnings of modern stage machinery. This contrivance, planned by Brunelleschi in 15th-century Italy, shows an 'angel' descending before Mary.

21

His wand pointing to Heaven, his back turned on Hell, a medieval impresario expounds the Miracle play of the Martyrdom of St. Apollonia.

Courtyards called 'corrales', which still survive in Spain, served as sites for the first, simple, secular stages – 400 years ago.

Title page for a Spanish 'auto sacramentale'. These religious medieval plays continued long after the birth of secular Theatre.

A Spanish actor, portrayed by a great Spanish artist: Velazquez

Italy led the way into the Renaissance, but soon the wealthiest power was Spain, with the gold of its American colonies at its command. Religious plays called *autos*, performed in Spain long before the Renaissance, continued to be performed long after it. But by the early sixteenth century, many Spanish writers came under Italian influence and produced both comedies of manners and romantic comedies, turning on the conflict between love and honor, that soon became an important characteristic of the Spanish Theatre.

Yet there were still no proper theatres. Strolling companies of the sixteenth century performed in cathedral-squares, market-places, and inn-yards. Cervantes, author of the famous *Don Quixote*, tells us how scanty their equipment was: their whole baggage going into a single sack, their stage consisting of a few planks laid across benches. But by the end of the century there were permanent theatres in Madrid, Seville and Valencia. Many had what we call the 'picture-frame' stage, with a proscenium arch and painted scenery. These theatres of the Spanish 'Golden Age' made use of

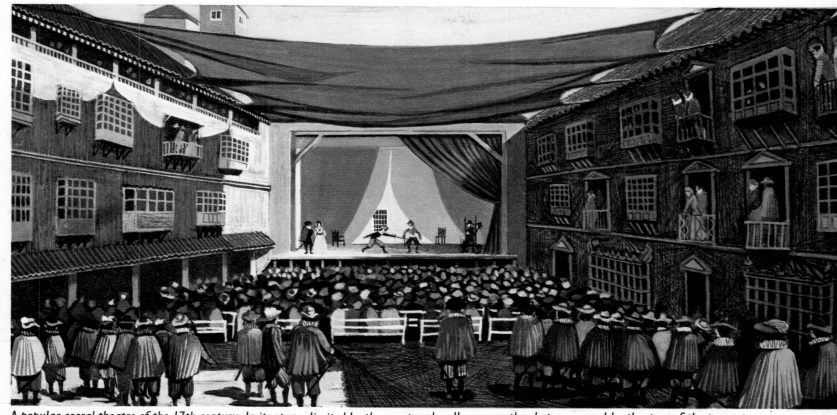

A popular corral theatre of the 17th century. In its stage, limited by the courtyard walls, we see the shape assumed by theatres of the present day. The seating arrangements designed for different levels of society hint at the pit, stalls, circle, boxes of the modern theatre.

the kind of stage with which we are all familiar, and this in turn gave the plays, which generally became divided into three acts, a familiar shape.

Life in Spain during this period offered the dramatists plenty of excellent material. It ran to extremes, from the stately magnificence of the Court and the nobles' palaces to the grim poverty of life in many country districts; from aristocratic and high-flown notions of honor to the cynical comic realism of the rogues and vagabonds.

During the first half of this 'Golden Age' the outstanding dramatist was Lope de Vega. It is estimated that he wrote at least fifteen-hundred plays, many of them in elaborate verse form. To satisfy the Spanish public's enormous appetite for drama he worked at high pressure, at times completing a play in a single day, with messengers from the stage manager waiting to carry off the sheets as soon as he had finished them. Yet his best remaining plays have genuine merit.

Towering above the many playwrights who came between him and Lope de Vega was Calderon, one of the world's great dramatic poets. Calderon was a master of stagecraft as well as the poet of sumptuous verse. He could turn with ease from allegory, from the religious parables of the *autos* which he never ceased to write, to powerful plays in

a realistic setting, like his *Mayor of Zalamea*. But his most valuable contributions to world drama are probably his deeply poetic plays, especially *The Wonderful Magician* and *Life is a Dream*. With Calderon this 'Golden Age' of the Spanish Theatre ends in a sunset blaze of glory.

23

Lope Felix de Vega Carpio (1562-1635). Nearly 500 of his tragi-comedies remain: plays owing little to the classic dramas of the past.

England's Elizabethan Theatre developed rapidly during the triumphant years following the defeat of the Spanish Armada. For some time, troupes of professional players, the retainers of wealthy nobles, had toured the country to increase their masters' prestige. There was also amateur performing of Moralities and knockabout folk-entertainment. The professional actor-managers – including Shakespeare – who eventually built and ran the London playhouses, still looked to the Court and important noblemen for their permits to perform, but they had to attract popular audiences. These wanted clowning and sword-combats, but had a genuine passion for quickness of wit and poetry spoken with fire and feeling.

The Elizabethan stage was admirably designed to please a quick-witted and imaginative audience. It consisted of a forestage, jutting into the audience, on which outdoor scenes were played; a curtained inner stage to suggest interiors; and an upper stage or balcony. Because there was no scenery to be changed, no curtain to be

Bear Garden and Globe vied for popularity on London's South Bank.

Best surviving 16th-century sketch of a London theatre: the Swan

lowered, the dramatist could move freely and swiftly from place to place. Having only words at his command for description of time, place and atmosphere, the dramatist had to use his imagination and compelled his audience to use theirs. All had to be done by the poet and the actors (who, including the boys who played the women's parts, were thoroughly trained and accomplished). As he delivered one of the famous speeches (written as great solos for the voice, like an *aria* in opera) the actor on the forestage had an intimate relation with his audience, perhaps impossible to recapture on our picture-frame stage. We put the actor in another world, at which we stare through the frame of the proscenium arch; Elizabethan Theatre brought the actor into our world, creating dramatic experience of a kind never since achieved.

(Left) By 1600, England's inn-yard stages had led to fine theatres like the Globe; where rich and poor, scholar and simpleton, thrilled to the plays of Shakespeare.

The best, known, painted likeness of William Shakespeare (1564–1616)

There is no room here fully to discuss the poetic genius of Shakespeare, the most gifted human being who ever put pen to paper. But, apart from silly theories that will not accept Shakespeare the actor as the author of the plays, there are two mistaken ideas about Shakespeare that must be mentioned.

The first, popular among the neo-classical critics of the eighteenth century, was that he was a kind of inspired barbarian, hardly knowing what he was doing. The second wrong view of him, which we owe to the romantic critics of the nineteenth century, suggests that every line he ever wrote is heavy with profound meaning, that he was infallibly wiser than we are, and incapable of careless writing.

Even if Ben Jonson had not told us that Shakespeare wrote his plays quickly, we could have guessed that he did simply because he wrote so much (besides acting and, later, helping to manage a company) in so short a time. Often he was careless and lost interest in what he was doing. Again, he preferred to take his plots from stories of older plays, and sometimes he got into a muddle because he put too much into a character for the part that character has to play in the action. In *The Merchant of Venice* Shylock becomes too human for the villainous part he has to play. Falstaff grew so much bigger and better than he was intended to be that Shakespeare had to 'kill him off' in *Henry V*. It is more than likely that the character of Hamlet has bewildered so many critics just because most of what he does belongs to an older play, whereas the superb things Hamlet says are very much Shakespeare himself.

He wrote always out of prevailing moods; and it is easy to discover what these were from the language, the sort of imagery, that he used. The plays show him to us beginning in confident high spirits, then doubting and questioning, then discovering depths of disgust and horror, finally recovering himself: taking it easy in his retirement, telling the romantic fairy stories of *The Winter's Tale* and *The Tempest*.

Having an extraordinary, rich nature, Shakespeare was divided and contradictory about many things. For instance, he believed in law and order and sober conduct and a sense of duty, but he could not help feeling some sympathy with rebellious and raffish characters, whether comic like Falstaff, or tragic like Antony and Cleopatra. But then he would not have been the supreme master of drama he was if he had not had this astonishing breadth of sympathy, creating contradictions and a tug-of-war in his mind.

Fool and hero find a place in Shakespeare's tragedy 'King Lear'.

Adornments to the first English version of 'Plutarch's Lives of the Noble Grecians and Romans'. Many Shakespeare plays retell its tales.

Queen Elizabeth and her Knights of the Garter at Windsor Castle: a scene of pomp and pageantry in England's great age of prosperity, progress and discovery—the age of Shakespeare—the vivid atmosphere that helped breathe life into each character, each scene of Shakespeare's plays.

Other dramatists bring important characters, big scenes to life; but Shakespeare can bring the smallest characters and the tiniest scenes equally to life. And though he often seems careless and casual, just flinging one little scene after another at us, more often than not he is building up his drama, with its own world, its own atmosphere, by one wonderful little stroke after another. It is this combination of unique breadth of sympathy and intense dramatic life that makes Shakespeare the supreme master of the Theatre of any age or any nation.

Shakespeare's and many others' characters found fame on London stages.

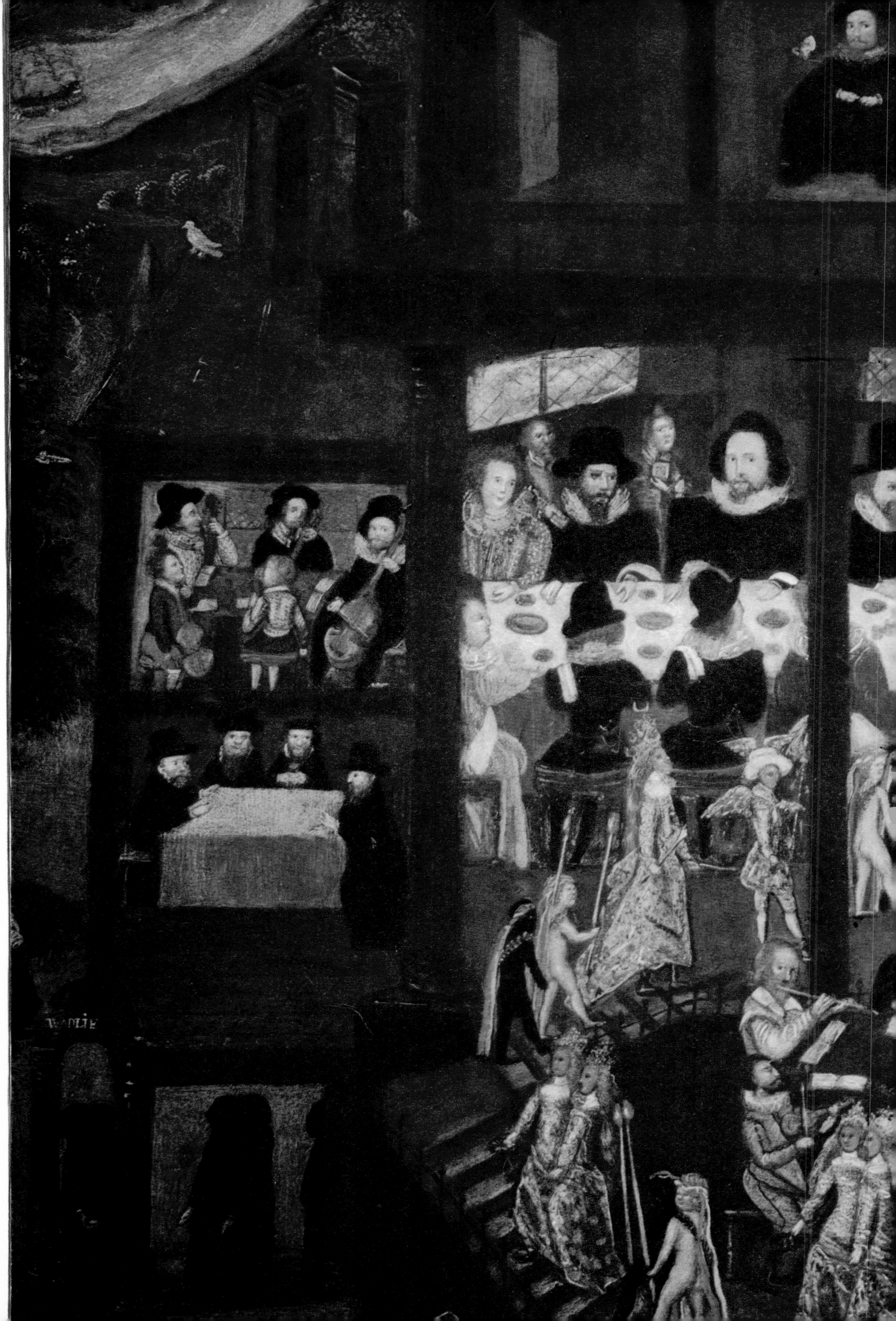

There was more dramatic talent in the London of Elizabeth and James I than there has ever been since in that city or any other. To name only a few: Marlowe, a tragic poet of strange wild power; Ben Jonson, whose best comedies are superbly written and crammed with rich speech; Dekker, excellent in comedy and in his romantic-pathetic women characters; Middleton and Heywood, with their bustling plays of contemporary life; the tragic and sinister Webster; Massinger, an adroit master of effective acting scenes; and Beaumont and Fletcher, ingenious, versatile and very successful.

But the real Elizabethan Theatre, with its packed pits, its comic breadth, its poetic grandeur, its tremendous vitality, had vanished before Shakespeare died in 1616. The old playhouses, unroofed and giving their performances only during daylight, had made way for covered theatres playing in the evening by the artificial light of candles.

Under James I there was not the same popular enthusiasm for the drama. The Puritans, rapidly increasing in numbers and influence, hated the Theatre which retaliated by burlesquing them and making the most of its threatened freedom. But the theatres closed by the Puritan Parliamentary Ordinance of 1642 had little of the vitality and value of the original Elizabethan Theatre.

As the drama proper declined during the reigns of James I and Charles I, the Masque claimed more and more attention. The Masque originated in renaissance Italy, and during the sixteenth century found its way first to the French, then to the English Court. It was essentially a court entertainment, designed to be what we should call now an 'after-dinner show' on splendid occasions. It had no real dramatic structure. Poets wrote complimentary verses to be spoken in it, but it mostly consisted of song-and-dance scenes, which, under the two Stuart kings, were often lavishly produced, being magnificently mounted and dressed.

By encouraging scene designers and painters, the use of rich and fantastic costumes, the invention of stage machinery, the Masque undoubtedly made possible the later production of opera and ballet. But if we regard the Theatre as the home of truly imaginative drama, the creator of real dramatic experience, the Masque did it more harm than good. For what it gave to the eye, what it did to satisfy the idle curiosity and wonder of its spectators, it took away from imagination.

The Masque: a recording on canvas of 16th-century showmanship

29

Proscenium

ædes

Theatrum

Fornices

From Venice to Weimar

In the period between 1650–1750 (often called 'neo-classical' as it copied the tastes of classical Rome) France, with its dominating position, and magnificent Court of Versailles, took the lead in the Theatre. But France owed a great deal to Italy. Two types of drama found their way into Italian Theatre: one scholarly, the other popular.

In fifteenth-century Italy, Greek scholars escaping from the Turks, settled and taught in academies. Generations ahead of the rest of Europe, Italy revived classical drama – especially Greek New Comedy and Latin imitations of it by Plautus and Terence. Famous Italian authors, notably Ariosto, Machiavelli, Bruno, wrote comedies based on classical models, though inventing characters of their own times. Satirical, topical writers showed what could be done with situations from ordinary life. Meanwhile Italian architects developed stages and auditoriums which led European theatrical design for two centuries.

The popular contribution came from the unique Italian *commedia dell' arte*, possibly the old Mime come to life again. Traces of it remain to this day in the Harlequinade and Punch-and-Judy. Its masked characters, played by women as well as men, were mostly stock comic figures: the foolish old man, swaggering soldier, interfering servants. *Commedia* dialogue was improvised by the quick-witted players. But scenes followed a definite plot.

This popular comic drama was imported into France, where an Italian company played for over a century. Thus on both scholarly and popular levels first credit must go to Italy for founding a neo-classical Theatre in Europe.

31

Inspired by Italy's classic past: a 16th-century court theatre

This Theatre gave us Molière, the world's greatest writer of classical artificial comedy. After touring the provinces for twelve years with his own company, Molière returned to Paris and was fortunate in obtaining the patronage of Louis XIV.

At this time a satirical dramatist in France was in a difficult position. If he offended the Court or the Church, the Theatre was closed to him and he might find himself under arrest. The Theatre owes something to Louis XIV for his patronage and protection of Molière; but if Molière had written in a freer society, his drama might have been even richer.

It was his duty to provide not only straight comedies but mixed pieces with songs and ballet. But his Theatre was not elaborate and spectacular; he worked mostly on a small and fairly simple scale, rarely with large casts, using the street and interior scenes common in this kind of comedy.

Molière has two outstanding qualities as a dramatist. The first is his inventive ingenuity, enabling him to make an effective comedy out of almost any fad or fashion. He was a wonderful contriver for the stage, giving every stroke its effect, every speech its sharp point. He knew his business as few dramatists have known theirs.

But it is his outstanding human quality that lifts him high above the other writers of artificial comedy. This quality comes from a kind of delicate balance in him of reason and feeling. Molière could create characters that may be taking part in a satire but for all that are not merely caricatures but have life and depth. Some of his more ambitious plays, such as *Le Misanthrope*, *Tartufe* and *Don Juan*, are far from being artificial comedies of the usual kind, having

The neo-classical French Theatre succeeded more in comedy than tragedy in an age which preferred to ignore those dark corners of the mind from which romantic literature emerges. It did not want a writer to record ideas private and peculiar to himself; it wanted him to express something everyone agreed about. All this helped satirical comedy, mocking absurd fashions and current affectations. The Theatre, entertaining a comparatively small Court society with frequent new satirical productions, is at such a time almost like a comic periodical.

Grief is unleashed as Italy's popular comedians depart from Paris.

Even courtly French comedy owed a debt to Italy's commedia dell' arte. Molière (extreme left) depicted playing an Italian farce.

much of the penetration and insight into life of the best serious drama. And even his lighter satirical pieces – sheer absurdities, burlesquing what seemed to him pretentious and inflated in the Parisian society he knew – never outrage as the plays of lesser comic playwrights do, the dignity and decency of life.

Desperately overworked and never in good health, unfortunate in his domestic life, responsible and anxious, Molière was far from being a happy man; but no man in his time, and very few since, brought as much wit and sparkling inventiveness into the Theatre and made so many others happy.

Playwright and actor, Molière (1622-73) was born Jean Baptiste Poquelin.

(Right) Old engraving of 'Le Malade Imaginaire'. (Left) Modern photo of 'L'Ecole des Femmes'. Unstaled by custom, the comedies of Molière remain as fresh as in his day.

LE
MALADE
IMAGINAIRE,
COMEDIE
MESLE'E DE MUSIQUE
ET
DE DANSES.
Par Monsieur de MOLIERE.

Corrigée sur l'original de l'Autheur, de toutes les fausses additions & suppositions de Scenes entieres, faites dans les Editions precedentes.

Représentée pour la premiere fois, sur le Theatre de la Salle du Palais Royal, le dixième Février 1673.
Par la Trouppe du Roy.

LE MALADE IMAGINAIRE

L ij

In costumes which reflected fashions of their day, French noblemen and women played Racine's 'ancient' tragedies at Louis XIV's Court.

French neo-classical tragedy in the seventeenth century was a drama governed by strict rules. The most important of these were the famous Unities, supposedly derived from Aristotle's *Poetics* but actually more severe than anything he had laid down.

It was decided that a true tragedy, obeying the Unities, would develop a single story (with no subplots), would use only one scene, and assume no greater passage of time than that taken by the play's performance. A further rule, less strictly observed, was that violent action should not be shown to the audience, but merely described to it.

Excellent drama, highly concentrated and tense, can be created within these rules. But the French classical theorists went wrong in imposing them on every tragic dramatist. They took much of the breadth and force and poetic grandeur out of tragedy – and indeed a great deal of its reality.

Jean Racine (1639-99) perfected plays written within the 'rules'.

Pierre Corneille (1606-84) wrote tragi-comedy outside the 'rules'.

The single scene became a vague antechamber, apparently belonging to nobody, too public for all the confidences exchanged in it. Often the time restriction meant so many crises happened close together that what ought to have been tragic became ludicrous. So much had to be described instead of seen that all the chief characters had to be provided with confidants and messengers – so many dummies in place of real characters. As tragedy must be kept high and mighty and not show or mention any homely familiar thing, significant details were missing from it, giving it an abstract, unreal air.

An additional problem was posed by the fashionable gentlemen, ever ready to titter or sneer at a dramatist who showed ignorance of the correct neo-classic rules, who occupied seats actually on the stage. They must have embarrassed the tragic poet and his actors.

But Pierre Corneille's most famous play, *Le Cid*, did not entirely conform to the rules and indeed Corneille, a romantic at heart, was never at ease with them. He had a good sense of the Theatre, though unless thoroughly roused by a big scene, a great moment, he could be prosy and rather tedious. But when challenged by that scene, that moment, his lines could be wonderfully sonorous and fiery.

Racine, much younger, was perfectly at home with the rules and even refined them, perfecting a poetic classical style, using plain language, yet with haunting cadences and undertones. He employed few characters, cut down the action to what was strictly necessary, but was searching and subtle in creating his chief characters, especially the women. Tragic actresses still covet the role of Racine's *Phèdre*.

His themes and personages are historical, but Racine makes little attempt to create the atmosphere of a period in history, to show us another age coming alive. It is hard to feel that these tragic characters are the Roman emperors and queens of Palestine we are told they are, and not eloquent ladies and gentlemen from the Court of Louis XIV.

Racine's Phedre, here played by the famous Sarah Bernhardt, is still a tragic role coveted by the leading actresses of France.

Neo-classic palaces and temples like this setting for Corneille's 'Andromède' dominated French stage designs 300 years ago.

(Left) The bewigged Congreve (1670-1729), fashionable playwright in a small court society. (Right) Oliver Goldsmith (1728-74), whose comedies appeared in an age of bigger, bourgeois audiences

The Duke's Theatre was opened on November 9th, 1671. Here played Sir William D'Avenant and the Duke of York's Company – one of two London companies granted patents to perform by Charles II.

The English Theatre began again soon after the Restoration of the Monarchy in 1660 when Charles II granted patents – permits to produce plays – to only two companies of players. When, much later, other theatres opened, their managers included song-and-dance scenes in their productions which were therefore not 'straight plays' needing a permit.

The two companies introduced actresses to play the female parts, and performed chiefly for the Court – the small, fashionable world. The Theatre was not rooted in national life as it had been under Elizabeth, and the wonderfully flexible Elizabethan stage had been replaced by the picture-frame stage on the Continental model.

The Restoration Theatre had its tragic dramatists, but the taste of the time made comedy far more important. There have been many critical disputes about these Restoration comedies. Some people condemn them for their monotony and indecency. Others consider them too artificial to be taken seriously as pictures of life and enjoy them simply as exhibitions of wit and comic character.

Wycherley, the coarsest, and perhaps the least witty of the early Restoration dramatists, is on the stage the most effective, for he had great dramatic vitality, and a fine eye for a droll character and an uproarious scene. But for style and wit, especially in his final comedy, *The Way of the World*, Congreve is the master of them all. In his best scenes, his brilliant style has never been surpassed in English comedy. The Theatre lost most by the early death of George Farquhar, whose *Recruiting Officer* and frequently revived *The Beaux' Stratagem* successfully broke away from the narrow artificial comedy of manners, took the scene from London into the country, and brought a breezy freshness into a comedy that was turning stale.

The English Theatre had to wait nearly seventy years for comedy as good as Farquhar's. Then came two Irishmen: Goldsmith and Sheridan. Goldsmith's first comedy, *The Good-Natured Man*, was a failure, but his second, *She Stoops to Conquer*, has triumphantly held the stage since its first appearance. Its central plot, a young man mistaking

a private house for an inn, was not original and is wildly unconvincing; but the play is written with such gusto that it still captivates audiences.

Sheridan, who in spite of being in politics contrived to manage Drury Lane for many years, wrote only two outstanding comedies, both while he was young: *The Rivals* and *The School for Scandal*. *The Rivals* has the fresher wit, the more unforced youthful gaiety, but *The School for Scandal* has been revived more frequently than any comedy written by any playwright since Shakespeare.

Merry-andrews, 'queens' and 'emperors' might fall, but Southwark Fair could still astonish and delight crowds which might never see inside the Duke's Theatre. Engraved by Hogarth, here are musicians, gamblers, tight-rope walking, 'Punch's Opera' and 'The Siege of Troy'.

The chief developments in European Theatre during the first three-quarters of the eighteenth century are a change in audiences and their taste, and revolt against dominating French influence, all-powerful during the early years of the century.

In Scandinavia, when by 1737 Stockholm had its Royal Theatre, French influence was still paramount; but Holberg, who directed the Danish Theatre, created a lively Danish-Norwegian style.

In Russia, French, German and Italian companies paid long visits and it was not until the last quarter of the century that a native Russian drama grew up. In Germany, visiting French companies played their classics at the larger courts, while German companies, playing popular stuff with plenty of clowning, amused the townsfolk. English companies, which had had a great reputation during the Elizabethan age, no longer toured Europe;

however, in 1752 the first professional London company crossed the sea to Williamsburg, Virginia, which, like New York, Philadelphia and Charleston, already had a playhouse of a sort.

Meanwhile, in London itself, the regular audiences were no longer merely composed of the upper class. The solid middle class, making up family parties, now patronised the playhouses; and these people did not want witty indecencies but plays with plenty of melodramatic action and sentiment. They were chiefly catered for by George Lillo, his greatest hit being *The London Merchant; or The History of George Barnwell* – an unfortunate youth who, falling in love with a bad woman, murdered his rich old uncle.

In Paris, the most famous author of the age, Voltaire, was creating a new fashion by writing 'tragedies', very different from Racine's, which demanded spectacular effects in exotic settings. It was his *Semiramis* that finally cleared once privileged spectators off the stage in France.

The new movement, then, responding to the change of audiences and taste, went in two directions. In one, it replaced artificial comedies by sentimental domestic plays appealing to middle-class families. In the other, it moved towards larger theatres with deeper, wider stages where, instead of formal tragedies, these new audiences were offered plays with plenty of action, numerous scenes, crowds of Incas, Aztecs, Chinese, Turks, and grand, spectacular effects including battle-scenes, temples on fire, waterfalls and rivers in glittering motion.

At the same time there were literary influences at work, destined to play an important part in the whole European Theatre. The first, and less important, was the publication of old ballads and folk-songs like Bishop Percy's *Reliques of Ancient English Poetry*. Particularly in central and northern Europe these encouraged a romantic taste for the past and for folk-poetry; a taste that was not destined to remain long outside the Theatre.

The second influence, of immense importance, was the discovery of Shakespeare by foreign scholars; then through their translations, by foreign dramatists, critics, actors and managers who found themselves staring into a whole new magic world of drama – tragic, comic, historical, fantastic. Young dramatists in one country after another (with Germany in the lead) became fascinated by this newly-revealed magic and found a new way, far removed from classical formality, of writing for the Theatre.

(Left) Scenic spectacle on the 18th-century stage could be contrived by pinning painted canvases to side-wings' wooden frames.

The Munich Altes Residenztheater: its ornate beauty was created solely to satisfy the tastes of German princes and their friends.

39

Theatres had to hold more, plays had to please more, as big merchant-class family parties replaced the select court audience.

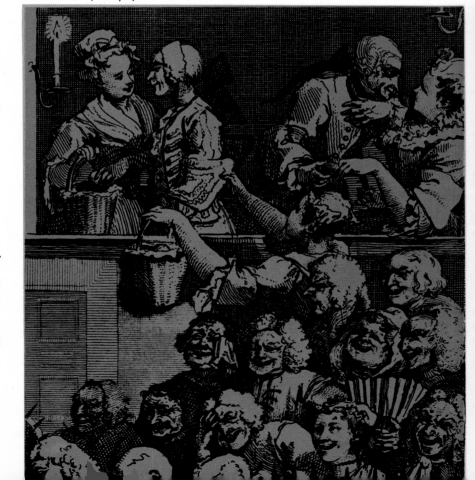

40

The English, Spanish and French Theatres reached their peaks during the century that began about 1590. At no time did the German Theatre reach such eminence, but towards the end of the eighteenth century it took the European lead.

The father of this Theatre was Lessing, himself both critic and dramatist. With his more important plays like *Minna von Barnhelm*, which dealt with contemporary German life, *Emilia Galotti*, a tragedy of middle-class life, and *Nathan the Wise*, a parable play about religious tolerance, Lessing awakened Germany to the possibilities of its Theatre.

Lessing's challenge was accepted by two poets of genius: Goethe and Schiller. After a wild start during what became called the *Sturm und Drang* – Storm and Stress – period (after a play of that name), they settled near each other and separately raised German poetic drama to a lofty height.

A sketch by Goethe (1749-1832) for his own mystic drama 'Faust'

Goethe, the foremost German writer, was appointed Minister of State by the Duke of Weimar and Director of the Duke's private theatre. This small dukedom was not wealthy. Goethe had to make the most of a badly-equipped playhouse, old scenery and costumes, and an inadequate company of undistinguished, overworked, underpaid players. Moreover, although Goethe wrote plays of wonderful poetic quality and had a fine taste in drama, he was not at heart a man of the Theatre. *Iphigenia* and *Torquato Tasso* are too slow moving, *Egmont* lacks true dramatic development, and *Faust*, though a literary masterpiece, makes too many demands upon the Theatre's resources. However, Goethe made little Weimar the capital of European Theatre.

Schiller, like Racine in France, has always had a greater reputation at home than abroad. For eloquent and firmly constructed historical tragedy, he was certainly unmatched in his romantic age. His most ambitious work, a trilogy of plays based on the life of Count Wallenstein, has never been widely played outside Germany, but his *Don Carlos*, *Maria Stuart*, *William Tell*, have taken possession of many stages in many countries. His dramatic virtues stem from his generous idealism, eloquence and feeling for theatrical effect. He lacks what Shakespeare possesses in abundance: a sense of poetic historical atmosphere and sharply individual characterisation.

The efforts of Goethe and Schiller at Weimar soon raised the level of the whole German Theatre which soon produced some fine dramatists. Ever since Goethe was at Weimar the Theatre has been firmly rooted in German national and civic life. No other country can show us so many well-organised and dignified municipal playhouses – excellent models for what ought to be done, but has not yet been seriously attempted, in America and Britain.

41

(Left) 'Romantic' Shakespeare drama inspired painting and plays.

Lessing (1729-81) helped German plays escape from classic 'rules'.

Drama in India died out when Moslem conquerors arrived but dramatic dancing (its every gesture holds a meaning) still survives.

Decorative and dramatic arts combine in this dancer and his dress.

42

Eastern Stages

Except in the Far East, the Asian peoples have not had a flourishing, highly-developed Theatre. This may seem surprising since they have devoted themselves to poetry, story-telling, singing, dancing and the decorative arts. There are two possible explanations. One is that Asia's monastic religions have attracted the types of thinkers who have created

Depicted on a 700-year-old frieze, the gestures of these temple dancing girls testify to the age-old traditions of Eastern art.

great drama elsewhere, and left them not free to consider the matter at all. The second, certainly true of India, is that the progress of drama was checked by Mohammedan invasions.

Hindu drama belongs to Sanskrit literature and it was an English translation of one of its classics (*Sakuntala*, by its best dramatist, Kalidasa) appearing in the late eighteenth century, that turned the attention of Europeans to Sanskrit literature. The origins of Hindu drama are not known. Possibly Greek invaders under Alexander the Great suggested the idea of drama; but it arrived at its best period, with Kalidasa, about the fifth century A.D.

Actors belonged to a special caste of no great dignity, and moved around with a leader; a kind of actor-manager who also introduced the play to the audience. There were no proper theatres and most performances took place, under the patronage of the local ruler, in a palace or temple. There was no scenery, just a curtain covering the back of the stage. Costumes and make-up were formal and traditional, indicating the caste, nationality, type of character. A few stage properties, some 'noises off' and similar simple effects were used.

The plays were mostly based on stories from familiar myths and legends. They contained quite

Rama and Lakshmana fight the demon Ravana. Such ancient themes from religious history and myth inspired India's Sanskrit plays.

a wide variety of characters and some charming touches of drama, but would seem to Western play-goers too literary; needing more intrigue, action and dramatic interest. But two of these old Hindu plays, *Sakuntala*, already mentioned, and *The Toy Cart*, have been produced with some success in Western playhouses. After a very long interval of neglect, this classical Sanskrit drama was translated into Bengali and revived. Now, both Indian and Western plays are produced in the Indian Theatre.

'Three Battles Against Lü Pu'. Made before 1800, a painting shows the dramatic mime, gorgeous attire and simple, symbolic scenery of China's classic stage – a stage perhaps unchanged in 700 years.

Symbolic Chinese scenery: (above) Pu-ch'eng, canvas city wall; Ch'e-ch'i, a 'carriage' flag; Ling-ch'i, Shuai-ch'i, commanders' standards and Men-ch'iang-ch'i, the banner representing 'army'

Will the traditional Chinese Theatre, which has reached us almost unchanged after many centuries, survive the Communist régime, hurrying to modernise and Westernise everything? We can only hope so, for this ancient Chinese art makes a highly original contribution to world Theatre.

Watching a traditional Chinese production we might at first be more sharply aware of its originality than capable of enjoying it. The orchestra, harsh and explosive to our ears, plays a great part in this Theatre, heightening the climaxes and setting the tempo for entrances and exits.

The elaborate costumes, and equally elaborate and far more startling make-up, are formal and traditional and indicate exactly who a character is. For instance, a famous brigand chief has a striking dark blue face, scarlet eyebrows and beard, and an extra pair of eyes painted below his own.

There is no scenery. The stage, projecting squarely into the auditorium, is curtained at back and sides – one side for entrances, the other for exits. Stage properties are few and simple but symbolic and highly conventional. A table and chair can represent anything from actual furniture to a fortress. Black flags indicate a high wind, flags with waves on them suggest water; an actor carrying an oar is imagined to be in a boat, one who brandishes a horse-whip is supposed to be riding a horse. To suggest an army entering a city, a few actors carrying large banners (symbolising military grandeur) march by a painted arch held up by property men, who, dressed in black and presumed to be invisible, are frequently busy on the stage.

When the audience is to imagine a change of scene, the actors walk round in a circle. This may happen many times because the plays are immensely

44

long and very episodic, capable of suggesting whole epics of adventure. It is here, in the length and looseness of structure, that the chief weakness of this Theatre lies. The dramatist's art hardly reaches its height in such immense, wandering melodramas, complete with morals and happy endings.

But in Chinese drama the actor's art is richly and wonderfully represented. Most of us who have seen Chinese actors have been entranced simply by their miming – for example, pretending to fight with swords in a dark room or to row a boat – and this is only part of their training which includes manipulation of the voice for tragic or comic purposes, and highly stylised gestures in which the wave of a finger may carry a weight of meaning. Actors playing female roles must be particularly skilled.

With this extremely conventional and simplified method of staging a play, there is little or nothing to distract attention from the actors. They are not only acting the scenes but creating the world in which the scenes are taking place.

There is much to be said for a Theatre of this kind, with staging so economical, flexible, imaginative. Remember we agreed from the first that there must be convention – an acceptance on one level of the spectator's mind that something represents something else – in the Theatre. The Chinese took this convention as far as it will go. Is it possible we have something to learn from them?

45

Symbolic make-up of a Chinese classic actor tells a Chinese audience who and what he represents. The gold upon his painted mask identifies him as a god. Costume and wig of green reveal he also plays a dragon's part.

A fresh 'mask' must be made for each performance: the actor paints it on his face. This stylised version of a monkey's visage adorns the Emperor of monkeys. A pheasant-feathered helmet proclaims him warlike.

Surprising as it may seem to those who do not know them, the Japanese are very theatrical. They are an excitable people pretending to be very calm; bringing to their whole national life a certain histrionic element. There is more than a hint of the Theatre in their conventional costumes, carefully arranged backgrounds and settings, and stylised ceremonies. And they are extremely fond of the Theatre itself, including modern plays imported from the West.

The national Theatre in Japan consists of three forms of drama: the *Nō*, the oldest, most distinguished and elaborate form; the *Kabuki*, or popular Theatre; and the marionettes. The *Nō* plays, partly religious in origin, traditional and highly conventional in style, essentially aristocratic, would seem to Western audiences like some small-scale ceremonial kind of opera. The orchestra and singers, seated on the not-very-large square stage, play a

'Flower-ways' which ran between the audience and stage, provided Kabuki actors with exciting entrances unknown in Western plays.

Mask for a Nō play, Japan's most ancient drama. Actors must train from infancy to master its complex, delicate and subtle gestures.

In contrast to the conventions of the stately Nō, Kabuki plays offered audiences exciting melodrama set in realistic scenery.

Women played all Kabuki parts until a ban. After 1680 male actors took their roles; even this charming Eastern 'actress' is a man.

great part in these performances. One device of these plays, disconcerting to a Western spectator, is to split the time-effect; keeping the action (for instance the approach of a new character) at the slowest of slow-motion speeds, while the orchestra and singers suggest rapidity and urgency. The women's parts are played by specially trained male performers. It is a drama for connoisseurs, simple enough in the stories it tells, but very elaborate and stylised in its ritual of performance.

The *Kabuki* Theatre, designed to entertain the mass of people who found the atmosphere of the *Nō* plays too rarefied, is very different. Its stage is not very high or deep, but is extraordinarily wide. On a 'runway' extending from it to the back of the auditorium, characters can make extremely effective entrances and exits. Scenes are solid and realistic, and many of the stage effects – for instance, a village on fire – would be the envy of Western stage managers. The acting, both in the heightened tragic manner and the realistic comic style, is very good indeed. The players, again with no women among them, do not wear masks, as the chief actors in the *Nō* plays do, but are heavily made-up. Incidental music is used rather as the theatre orchestra used to be in nineteenth-century Western melodramas. *Kabuki* performances last much longer than ours and frequently scenes from several plays are given. Though Western drama is increasingly popular, new *Kabuki* plays, based on the old traditional stories, are still being written.

The third Japanese form, the marionettes, must not be confused with the kind of puppet-show familiar to us. The dolls are almost lifesize figures, very elaborately articulated; and each important one requires three trained men to manipulate it. Though these are visible, it is not difficult even for a Western newcomer to ignore their existence and to concentrate on the astonishingly graceful and significant movements and gestures of these marionette characters. The stage, much smaller than the *Kabuki* stage, is quite elaborately set, and its scenery is designed to enable the manipulators and their marionettes to move along different levels. The action of the pieces they perform is described by five singers accompanied by stringed instruments. But there is far less popular interest in this highly artificial type of Theatre and the very rapid development of film production in Japan is itself a threat to all three forms of the traditional Japanese Theatre.

47

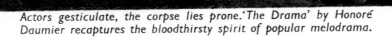

Actors gesticulate, the corpse lies prone.'The Drama' by Honoré
Daumier recaptures the bloodthirsty spirit of popular melodrama.

Romance and Realism

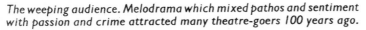

The weeping audience. Melodrama which mixed pathos and sentiment
with passion and crime attracted many theatre-goers 100 years ago.

The first half of the nineteenth century was on the whole a curiously uneventful period in the history of the European Theatre. It is typical of the earlier part of this age that the new plays most widely and successfully produced were those of a German, Kotzebue, whose work is now forgotten. They were in fact large spectacular melodramas adroitly contrived to please the taste of the popular audiences, and to show off the many resources of the big theatres these audiences filled. These pieces, which usually had an exotic setting, had neither literary nor true dramatic merit but were what is commonly known as 'good Theatre'.

It was not that real poets and men of talent had no interest in the Theatre. Several of the English romantic poets for example wrote plays, of which the best is probably Shelley's *Cenci*; but somehow they failed to achieve an essential theatrical quality; failed just as mysteriously as the Elizabethan and Jacobean poet-playwrights had succeeded.

Plays about the past led to 'authentic' copying of its costumes.

Great actors like Edmund Kean in London, Talma in Paris, appeared in revivals of the classics and helped raise the art of acting to a new high level. But drama itself made no progress, in spite of what Goethe and Schiller had accomplished.

Nothing momentous happened in the Theatre until a famous night in 1830 when Victor Hugo's *Hernani* was first produced and caused a riot. Hugo had deliberately broken all the rules of classic restraint and, knowing there would be trouble, took care to bring into the theatre four hundred enthusiastic young men, art students and the like, who supported the new romantic attitude.

Hugo was a greater poet than playwright, but his act of rebellion brought new life to the French Theatre. So did the exciting historical melodramas of Dumas; though soon to be excelled by those of his son, Dumas *fils*, the author of the famous 'tear-jerker' *The Lady of the Camellias*. Less successful at first than any of these, but really a more interesting dramatist, was the poet Alfred de Musset, whose delicate, half-romantic, half-mocking pieces came to be played and enjoyed more and more during the latter half of the century, when the Theatre everywhere gained vitality.

'Hernani', set in the romantic past, horrified 'classic' critics.

(Left) Victor Hugo (1802–85) led France's romantic revolt in drama. (Middle) Victorien Sardou (1831–1908), famed more for inventing melodramatic plots than lifelike characters. (Right) Eugène Scribe (1791–1861) contrived 'well-made' plays to delight middle-class audiences.

Seated in a box on that riotous first night of Hugo's *Hernani*, a prominent member of the group opposing the poet, was Eugène Scribe. He became the most popular playwright of the period 1830–1860, and, with a number of collaborators, is said to have written four hundred plays. Scribe was the originator of what was known as the 'well-made' play, and he and his successor, Victorien Sardou, dominated the commercial Theatre in France and elsewhere during the nineteenth century. It was a Theatre that set out to entertain the comfortable bourgeois classes, on the increase in all the capitals. These audiences were not necessarily foolish, but lacked imagination and never expected the Theatre

'An Entr'acte at the Comédie Française' shows the stiff-shirted audience whose patronage gave many theatres the shape they bear today.

'Kean': a French play about a great 19th-century English actor

to tell them anything worth knowing about life.

The trouble with these Scribe-Sardou plays is that they are so much adroit construction and contrivance and little else. They do not spring out of living characters and their circumstances. They are merely clever concoctions in which effective scenes, startling situations, are thought of first and fitted out with dummy characters.

But right to the end of the nineteenth century, this type of play, usually staged and acted with considerable skill, took possession of the smaller and more expensive playhouses everywhere; leaving the spectacular melodramas, which for all their crudities had often more dramatic vitality in them, to the larger theatres with plenty of cheap seats in the pit and gallery.

It was these smaller playhouses, designed to attract audiences of the middle and upper classes, that about the middle of the century made changes which helped to create the playhouse as we know it today. In the old theatres were no 'orchestra stalls' or '*fauteuils*', now the most expensive seats in the house. The pit, farther below stage level than the stalls are today, occupied the whole floor of the theatre; and the best seats were in the first circle, not then much above stage level. But the new, smaller, more fashionable playhouses pushed the pit to the back, often reducing it to a few rows, and filled the area between it and the stage with comfortable, numbered stalls that could be booked by theatre-goers in advance.

The large old popular theatres had offered a long, mixed entertainment, often with a full-length play, a few songs, and a short farce as a final item. The new playhouses opened later in the evening, and though a short piece called a 'curtain raiser' might precede the play, the interlude of singing and the final farce were dropped. Because their chief patrons now arrived in evening-dress, these new and more expensive theatres were made cleaner, more comfortable and better ventilated than the big popular theatres had ever been.

As industrial wealth increased throughout the century, so these more luxurious commercial playhouses multiplied on both sides of the Atlantic. But with these theatres disappeared that heightened feeling of being one in an audience; a communal, classless feeling which the big old theatres had known. It needed more than theatre-going as a social habit to restore vitality to the drama.

Sir Henry Irving as Shakespeare's Richard III. Great actors, perhaps more than playwrights, drew Europe's biggest audiences

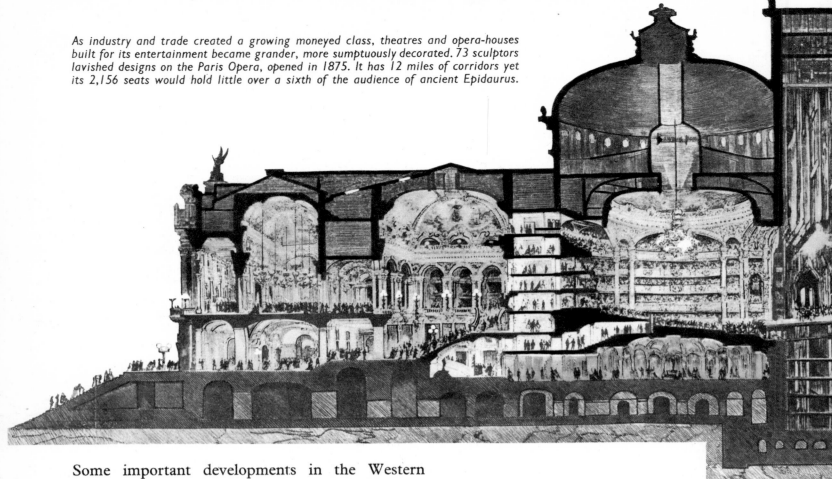

Some important developments in the Western Theatre can be illustrated by what happened in London in the 1860s. Tom Robertson, a dramatist who had been an actor, joined forces with Squire Bancroft, an accomplished actor, and his wife, Marie Wilton, an extremely popular actress.

Robertson supplied these two, who were also theatre managers, with a series of plays (*Society, Ours, Caste, Play, School*) that were called 'cup-and-saucer' drama because they avoided wildly dramatic scenes, huge flowery speeches, fantastically unreal characters in impossible situations; and successfully attempted a far more realistic type of domestic, sentimental, humorous drama. This was directed with great care by Robertson himself.

Actors, receiving much larger salaries than had been customary, were carefully selected to play particular parts, and rehearsed for some weeks. All this was new. Before, actors had formed part of a stock company, playing many different parts. Rehearsals were few and casual; only the major movements and groupings were worked out, and an experienced actor was assumed to know what to do with himself on the stage.

Robertson insisted on the setting of his plays being realistic: a room had to be exactly the kind of room he described in his text. It could no longer be a large, vague, bare apartment, unconvincingly put together out of side-pieces or 'wings' and a back-cloth. It had to look like somebody's room, not nobody's; it had to have walls; it had to be properly decorated and furnished; it had to have doors and windows that opened. This meant the use for all interiors of 'box sets' made up of canvas 'flats' cleated together to form the three walls, of a ceiling and of practicable doors and windows.

The old painted-cloth-and-wings room may not have looked attractive or convincing (do we go to the Theatre to see rooms anyway?) but it never had a piece of furniture that was not essential for the action, it cost very little, would do for almost any play, and could be changed in half a minute. Its painted cloths were 'flown': hoisted into the 'flies' where men, hidden by the proscenium arch, raised and lowered the scenery high above the stage.

The old painted-cloth scenery made repertory easy and inexpensive. It cost little to change plays every night for a week. But the introduction of these box sets, heavily furnished and 'dressed' (as stage managers say) with pictures, ornaments, clocks, etc., made repertory difficult and costly. Men like Robertson and Bancroft were preparing for a long run of one play, not for the continuing production of a number of plays. This new realism then, so far as

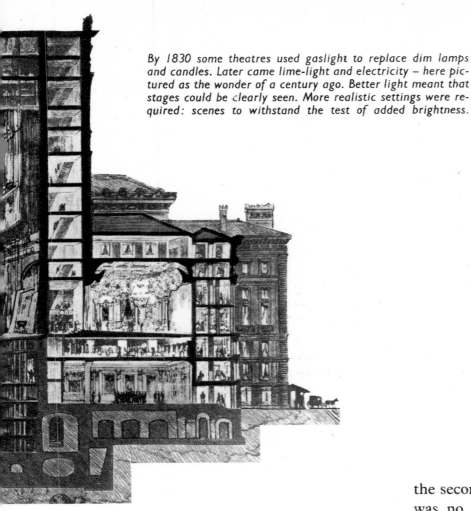

By 1830 some theatres used gaslight to replace dim lamps and candles. Later came lime-light and electricity – here pictured as the wonder of a century ago. Better light meant that stages could be clearly seen. More realistic settings were required: scenes to withstand the test of added brightness.

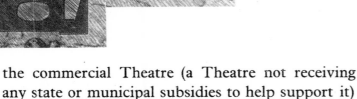

the commercial Theatre (a Theatre not receiving any state or municipal subsidies to help support it) was concerned, almost brought repertory to an end.

As both costs of production and salaries went up, and only a long run brought any profit, managers soon showed less and less desire to be adventurous and experimental in their choice of plays. During the second half of the century the most vital drama was no longer making its first appearance in the wealthiest cities – in London, New York or Paris, where more and more commercial theatres came into existence, producing well-tried plays 'adapted from the French' of Scribe and Sardou.

Yet, ironically enough, this new drama had not turned away from realism or naturalism in the Theatre, but simply raised it to a higher power.

53

The Crimean hut: a realistic scene from Tom Robertson's 'Ours'; no longer contrived from unconvincing wings but built up by a box set

August Strindberg's plays echo the semi-dreamworld of his mind.

Henrik Ibsen: his plays pose, not solve, life's serious problems.

This new drama came, most unexpectedly, from Norway. Henrik Ibsen (1828–1906), as a young Norwegian beginning to write plays, worked in the Theatre at Bergen and Oslo, received a fellowship, then a state pension but lived out of Norway in Italy and Germany, for most of his life.

He was always at heart a poet; and two of his most important earlier dramas, *Brand* and *Peer* *Gynt*, do not belong to the Theatre of prose realism. But most of his work does, and his tremendous influence on world, as well as Norwegian Theatre, has been as a dramatist of prose realism.

Ibsen's contribution to the Theatre was two-fold. He brought to it a deeply searching and serious mind. The issues in an Ibsen play are in fact the most serious issues known to the modern mind.

The Master Builder falls from a steeple unseen by the audience; for in Ibsen's plays ideas matter more than mere melodramatic spectacle.

Although he had a natural inclination towards a poetic and symbolic treatment, he realised that the Theatre of his time was committing itself more and more to realism or naturalism, and in his own determined, grimly patient fashion – for he was a grim, determined man – he hammered out a realistic prose technique that beat the Theatre at its own game.

This brings us to his second contribution. He took the 'well-made' play, charged it with high seriousness instead of triviality, and made it technically even better. He did it by a severe concentration of the action. Instead of showing his characters in a series of scenes leading to a crisis as other dramatists had done, he began his most characteristic plays just before the crisis arrived, made his audience acquainted with what had gone before by talk – dramatic in itself – between his characters, and then devoted the main part of his play to a resolving of the crisis.

This method gave an Ibsen drama a richness and dramatic urgency immensely rewarding to audiences prepared to use their intelligence and release their emotions, distasteful to this day to people who merely want to giggle or doze in the playhouse.

Though Ibsen's originality and greatness cannot be questioned, he has limitations. His characters share Ibsen's humorless nature; and his creation of character, though searching and profound, is rather narrowly based for the greatest dramatist of his age.

Oddly enough, the only possible challenge to his pre-eminence also comes from Scandinavia, in the person of August Strindberg (1849–1912), a Swede. Strindberg may have learnt some of his fine technique from Ibsen, but their plays are very different. A far more unbalanced man, close to insanity at times, Strindberg is more unequal than Ibsen, though also even more versatile. In certain of his plays, like *The Father*, within a convincingly realistic framework he can produce drama of almost appalling intensity; in some plays his psychological subtlety is even superior to Ibsen's.

Both dramatists are held to have brought into existence the 'problem' play. But a great dramatist does not solve 'whodunnit' problems. He may create for us a certain kind of dramatic experience involving religious, philosophical, social or political issues which are an important part of our lives, but he leaves us to settle these problems ourselves.

55

(Left) The playwrights Anton Chekhov (1860–1904) and Maxim Gorki (1868–1936): two Russian masters in the art of writing realistic drama. (Right) The stage director Konstantin Stanislavski (1863–1938) co-founder of the Moscow Art Theatre and one of its great actors

Realism for realism's sake probably reached its peak with the New York manager, David Belasco, who thought nothing of putting an exact replica of a restaurant on the stage. But this was showmanship.

The finest examples of complete naturalism – interpreting the play's texts – could be found in Moscow in the early years of this century. They were the productions of the Moscow Art Theatre, founded in 1898 by Stanislavski and Nemirovich-Danchenko, who were both dissatisfied by the artificial style of acting then existing in Russia.

Older realistic playwrights like Ostrovski needed a less mannered style of acting; and promising new writers like Chekhov could not be properly produced at all in the existing manner. Two visits by the Meiningen Company from Germany, famous for its settings, crowd-acting and the accuracy and finish of its productions, had convinced many Russians that new theatrical companies, methods of training actors and staging plays were needed. The Moscow Art Theatre was easily the greatest of these new companies, and it still is.

It will always be associated with the name of Chekhov, one of the most original and subtle of all dramatists. He disregarded every rule of playwriting. He is not telling anybody's story. He is not showing a conflict between determined characters. Instead of having more will-power than most of us, his characters have less.

There is no conflict, no crisis, no climax. He says in effect, 'This is what life was like to this group of people'. In place of the familiar dramatic excitement he gives us a wonderful depth of character and scene: humorous, pathetic, tender. When his people

'The Blue Room' designed by Dobujinsky – scene from a Moscow Art Theatre production of Ivan Turgenev's play 'A Month in the Country'

Exotic East as well as realistic West found a flourishing place in Russian culture around 1900: Goncharova's design for Rimsky Korsakov's drama-in-music 'The Golden Cockerel'.

are eloquent, they are merely showing off and being silly. When they truly reveal themselves, they do it in a few casual, broken phrases.

It is the only drama that seems to have more inconsequence than real life. But it is composed with consummate art. Its naturalism is a poetic naturalism. This is the key to the Moscow Art Theatre productions of Chekhov; built up slowly, with great elaboration.

All manner of effects are introduced – a bird singing, a train passing, distant music, and so forth – but not for reality's sake. Like the beautiful lighting of these plays, they create atmosphere, heighten the emotion of a scene, 'orchestrate' the author's text.

In these Moscow Art Theatre productions of Chekhov with their special training of actors, endless rehearsals, immense care for every detail of the sets, costume, make-up, intricate blending of speech and movement, lighting effects, the Theatre reached the summit of naturalism. This was not showmanship but an attempt to suggest inside the Theatre the wealth of sight and sound, the sudden humor, the hidden heartbreak, the largely unspoken poetry of this life of ours.

After 1900 Russian art, once remote from the Western world, enriched its stage costumes and designs: dance costume by Leon Bakst for ballet music by the French composer Debussy.

'Na dne' ('The Lower Depths'): an early Moscow Art Theatre production of Gorki's play shows real rags and filth which turn a stage into a cellar, realistic dismal misery of the actors – types of stage realism which reflect the mode of life of Russian poor when Gorki wrote.

Ideas and Experiments

So far during this century the Theatre has shown us a great deal of experiment and an increasing variety of styles – in writing, stage design, acting and production – rather than a continued development of one style, as in earlier centuries.

Non-commercial and experimental theatrical companies have been dominated far more by directors and dramatists than by star actors managing their own companies. For instance, the famous Abbey Theatre in Dublin was run first by W. B. Yeats, a great poet, and Lady Gregory, a playwright, and afterwards by Lennox Robinson, another playwright. This was essentially a national Theatre, designed to produce Irish drama; and it gave us such fine dramatists as Synge and Sean O'Casey. In America, the Provincetown Players were associated with Eugene O'Neill, then a young dramatist.

In Germany and Russia during the 1920s the Theatre was wildly experimental, making a clean break both in writing and production with realism. In Berlin there was much enthusiasm for a style called Expressionism, in which the characters were very broad types (called simply 'The Man' or 'The Girl') and the action was symbolic, dream-like and not realistic. In Paris new groups abandoned the style of the Boulevard playhouses for the sensitive realism of plays by Vildrac and Jean-Jacques Bernard, or the poetic drama of André Obey.

The greatest British dramatist, Bernard Shaw, experimented only in the subject-matter of his plays; and although some producing groups tried experiments for special performances, there was less breaking away from realism in London than in most other capitals.

Though the passion for experiment-at-all-costs of Berlin and Moscow in the 1920s has not been duplicated elsewhere, during the last twenty years there has been a gradual broadening, with T. S. Eliot and Christopher Fry succeeding with poetic drama, and with Arthur Miller and Tennessee Williams in New York, Giraudoux, Sartre, and Anouilh in Paris – all trying new forms of prose drama; giving apparent realism a poetic intensity. But no unique style has been developed that completely represents and essentially belongs to our age.

20th-century Theatre has produced not one but many new types of play, with fresh ideas put together in unfamiliar, experimental ways by the dramatists of many nations. Pictured on this page are portraits of three famous modern playwrights: (above) Italy's Luigi Pirandello (1867–1936), (middle) Britain's Bernard Shaw (1856–1950), (below) United States' Eugene O'Neill (1888–1953).

(above) scenes from 'Six
Characters in Search of an
Author' – Pirandello's
strange play asks the real
meaning of reality. A man's
character has many aspects.
Which is his real self? How
can one actor portray a
character of many selves?

(right) Bernard Shaw used
stage realism to publicise
social problems. Even
'Fanny's First Play', a farce,
contrasts the everyday dress
once worn by rich and poor.

One scene: New England,
one atmosphere: ancient
Greece, for in 'Mourning
Becomes Electra' Eugene
O'Neill turns from modern
realism to ancient myth. Inspired by Aeschylus he re-
tells the Oresteia legend,
aided by a chorus of old men.

(Above) Adapting experiments by Craig and Appia, stage designers create simple acting-backgrounds rather than scenic spectacles.

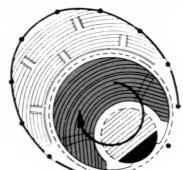

(Below) Invented in Russia in the 1920s, the acting levels of constructivist stage sets often resembled a half-assembled house.

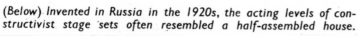

Early in this century revolt against realistic painted sets was led by two designers of great talent: Gordon Craig, an Englishman and Adolphe Appia, a Swiss. Both abolished fussy realistic detail, made their sets symbolic in form and coloration and tried to give their actors different levels on which to perform. Other directors and designers began to substitute solid three-dimensional shapes, often quite unrealistic, for painted cloths.

In the wildly experimental Theatre of Soviet Russia during the 1920s, a director called Meierhold devised a fantastic style known as 'Constructivism'. All suggestion of realism was replaced by ladders, bridges, bits of machinery, as if the stage designer had nothing to work with but a giant meccano set.

Europe's smaller experimental theatres made more and more use of the Elizabethan forestage or 'apron'. Especially in Shakespearean productions, playhouses with conventional stages used permanent sets that could suggest indoor and outdoor scenes by small changes like drawing a curtain.

Another method was to have nothing on the stage but a semicircular stretched cloth or a plaster cyclorama at the back. On this a camera would project scenes painted on slides. But such scenes tend to look thin and unconvincing.

In modern plays demanding rapid changes of scene, directors often used a 'multiple set' with several small interior or even exterior scenes; and picked out with spot-lights the part of the set in use, keeping the rest as dark as possible.

Today most large new theatres have either revolving stages, which simply swing into view the scene to be used, or machinery to raise and lower a large central section of the stage.

We do not go to the playhouse to stare at stage sets but to watch actors and listen to words; so there is something to be said for arena playhouses, or theatres-in-the-round, where the picture-frame notion of the stage is replaced by a stage like the ring of a circus, with no scenery at all. Its advantages lie in its inexpensive working, its intimate relation between actor and audience, and its increased demand upon the imagination of the spectators.

There are now stages which can become picture-frame stages, part picture-frame with forestage or steps going down to the audience, or not picture-frame at all but close replicas of the Elizabethan stage – three theatres for the price of one.

61

Architect Walter Gropius' 'Total Theatre': revolving floor could create arena-stage, cinema, opera-house – even a sports stadium.

'The Method' helps to teach New York's student actors to identify their inner feelings with those of the characters they portray.

There are many illusions about the Theatre among people who have never worked in it. One is that what happens on the stage is improvised, as if actors and actresses performed in a kind of charade. Actually in a serious production the smallest movement, the shortest speech, is carefully rehearsed.

Another illusion is that while acting might be very difficult to the ordinary man, it is very easy for a man born to be an actor. Ability to imitate a voice, a walk, a gesture, is often thought to be enough to make a man an actor. Though there have been great actors with little formal training, most actors nowadays were once students in drama schools.

There they learnt how to use their voice, how to speak clearly, how to control their breathing. They were taught good body-movements; how to walk, to sit down and get up, to dance, to fence. In advanced schools they learnt to observe and interpret character. In all the schools, before their two- to four-year courses were finished, they would have done some real acting; often competing for awards and prizes.

Each great capital city has several dramatic schools, some attached to particular theatres, like the Comédie Française in Paris. London's largest dramatic school, the Royal Academy of Dramatic Art, is not attached to any dramatic company but to

Actors at a fencing class learn not only special skill for use in historic dramas but suppler body-movement for everyday performance.

Dramas with special conventions need adaptable actors. Expressive 'Method'-trained faces are wasted when masks proclaim character.

London University. Russia's Moscow Art Theatre runs its own state-supported school where students selected from all over the vast Soviet Union study for four years. Here the more advanced instruction is based on methods devised by the co-founder of the Moscow Art Theatre, Konstantin Stanislavski, himself a magnificent actor.

The Actors' Studio in New York, which teaches 'The Method', has been much influenced by Stanislavski. This style of acting aims at extreme naturalism and is better suited to realistic contemporary plays than to the stylised classics. 'The Method' teaches the actor to identify himself inwardly with the character he has to play; to work from this inner identification to outward signs of character – tricks of voice, gait and gesture. This reverses the more general actor's procedure. Each system works well if it suits the actor's temperament. What must be remembered is that acting, like everything belonging to the Theatre, has a double aspect: the actor must be the character he is playing and also himself.

Without some truth to life, the costume comedy would not be engrossing: without some theatrical artificiality, the realistic play could not hold our attention. The Theatre must always be what we should never be – two-faced.

63

Present-day emphasis is more on actors, less on scenery: vivid costumes stress speech and gestures of players from France's 'T.N.P.'.

There are two ways of running professional theatrical enterprises. The first, and much the older, is associated with the world's most famous theatrical companies such as the Comédie Française, the Burgtheater in Vienna, the Moscow Art Theatre, the Old Vic. This system involves a permanent producing organisation which controls a theatre and engages its actors to perform in many plays.

In these companies, once a play has been thoroughly rehearsed and performed for several nights it goes into the *repertoire* of productions ready to be put on at any time. For this reason such companies are often called 'repertory companies'. In England, where many towns have so-called 'repertory companies', the term is wrongly used. These companies, producing one play for a run of one to three weeks, have in fact no *repertoire*. They are really 'stock companies'.

Being a member of a true repertory company can be hard on a lazy actor, who may be playing five parts in one week and has to rehearse old productions or create new ones. But for actors who

The few actors in a commedia dell' arte company produced their own plays, raised their own stages, designed their own costumes.

A simplified diagram hints at the complex behind-the-scenes organisation of the Moscow Art Theatre, a giant 20th-century company.

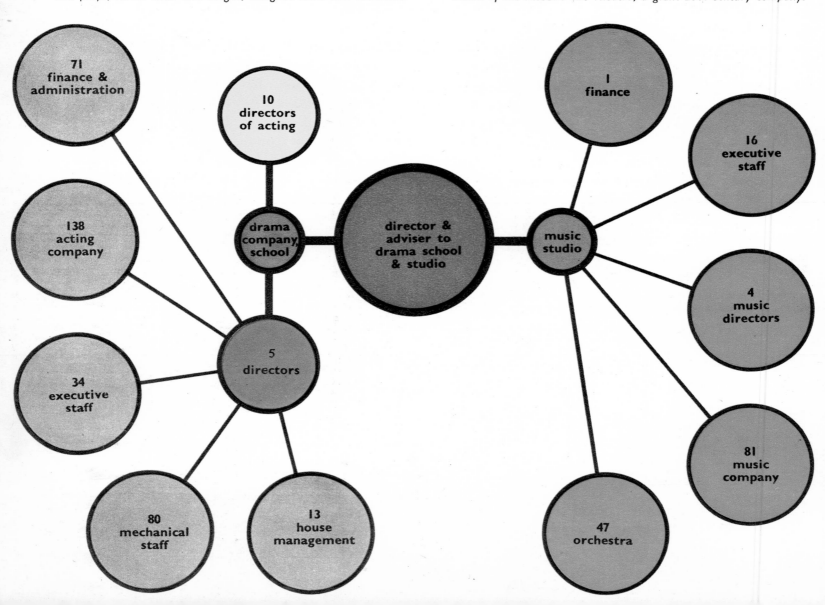

Modern equivalent of old strolling players, the small company of France's Théâtre National Populaire performs in ancient châteaux.

love their profession, this is the better system. It enables them to display their versatility, prevents them going stale, and makes good acting easier, like playing regularly with a team.

Though it is expensive to maintain a large company with scenery and costumes for many productions, less money is wasted than with the other system.

This, which might be called the *ad hoc* system, is the one employed by the commercial theatres of London, Paris, New York and many other capitals. A manager (called in New York a 'producer') decides to do a play. He employs a director, a scene-designer, a stage staff and actors – simply to do this one play. It may run only two weeks or two years. The one great advantage of this system is that it offers playwright and director a wide choice of actors and actresses. It encourages 'type-casting': finding an actor exactly right in type for a part.

In all other respects it is inferior to the permanent company and repertory system. A very short run is bad for everybody. A very long run is bad for actors and audiences; for if actors get stale audiences see a mechanical performance.

The overall waste of money on sets and costumes is appalling. No acting teams are built up. The system does not form part of a plan, as in countries where state companies have to tour the provinces for so many weeks a year. Expensive or difficult productions which would succeed as one play in a repertory, are never produced if they would fail as a long run performed by an 'ad hoc company'.

So although there is room in large cities for several commercial managements hoping for long runs, unless these are balanced by an equal number of non-commercial repertory companies, the Theatre will not be in a very healthy condition.

Many actors – yet but a small part of the army of administrators, designers and electricians composing the famous Comédie Française.

During the last thirty years the Theatre has had to meet three challenges – from radio, cinema, and television. All three produce drama of a sort; all possess important advantages.

As a rule it does not cost as much to see a film as it does to see a play; and films can be seen in a great many places that have never known a theatre. Radio and television can be enjoyed at home, with a minimum of effort, turning the living-room into a playhouse. And all three, because they are produced for a mass audience, can offer casts of players that only the best theatres could afford.

Outside America it is doubtful if the Theatre yet has had to meet all the competition that television drama can offer it, for this new form of drama is only in an early fumbling stage of its career. But already many people tell us that with their television sets at home and an occasional visit to the movies, they no longer need the Theatre and do not care whether it lives or dies.

Bird's-eye view of an intimate drama performed for television: Theatre's formidable, mass-medium rival, attracting a massive audience

Such people do not understand that the Theatre is the parent of these new dramatic forms. Without a living Theatre where writers, directors, designers and actors could learn their jobs, movies and television plays would be very crude indeed. Unfortunately the wealthy organisations responsible for films, radio and television, have helped themselves liberally to the talent the Theatre has trained but have given it little in return. In fact their competition has made the position of the Theatre which has no state support far more precarious than it used to be, and has made commercial theatre managers more reluctant than ever to experiment.

However, as these mass-media do some things better than the Theatre, they might be said to be narrowing but purifying its outlook. An obvious example is the disappearance from the stage of the old spectacular melodrama with its sinking ships, houses on fire, horses racing – simply because this can all be done much better by the film studios.

But there are equally important and more subtle results of this competition. For instance, because the best film dialogue tends to be laconic and rather dry, a certain richness of speech has returned to the Theatre, thus making the most of what it does best.

Again, though television drama is still in its infancy, it is clear that what succeeds most in this medium is drama consisting of intimate scenes between two or three characters; carefully rather than richly written and acted. It is happier with rather small but intensely sincere parts and performances than with extremes of comedy and tragedy acted by impressive personalities.

The Theatre can afford certain grandiose qualities that seem embarrassing in the cold searching light of television. We may expect, then, that quiet, intimate naturalism in writing and acting will appear more and more in television drama, and less and less in the Theatre which will begin to recover its old swagger and style and larger-than-life character.

A spectacle of ancient Rome revived for the spectacular film 'Ben-Hur'. Theatres no longer compete with the cinema's superior realism.

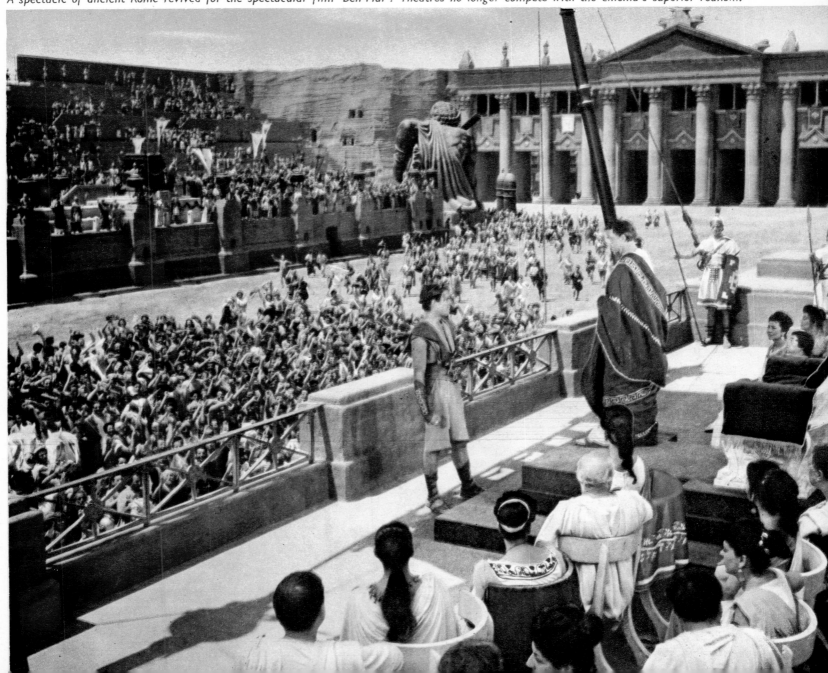

'Theatre' is found as much in simple village hall as in palatial city opera-house: in fact wherever actor meets audience face to face.

In a very good restaurant we have a dinner that is specially cooked for us; in a canteen we are merely served with standard portions of a standard meal. And this is the difference between the living Theatre and the mass entertainment of films, radio and television. In the Theatre the play is specially cooked for us. Those who have worked in the Theatre know that a production never takes its final shape until it has an audience.

With films, radio, television, the vast audience can only receive what it is being offered. But in the Theatre the audience might be said to be creatively receptive; its very presence, an intensely living presence, heightens the drama.

The actors are not playing to microphones and cameras but to warmly responsive fellow-creatures. And they are never giving exactly the same performance. If the audience tends to be heavy, unresponsive – on a wet Monday, perhaps – the company slightly sharpens and heightens its performance to bring the audience to life; and vice versa if the audience is too enthusiastic.

It is the presence of an audience that teaches an actor the essential art of 'timing'. If in comedy the speeches are badly timed; if the actors try to get too many laughs instead of checking little laughs in order to build up to a huge roar, the keen edge of the audience's attention will be obviously blunted, and the production will not succeed. An actor with talent and long experience always has a wonderful sense of what can be done with an audience; half commanding and half cajoling it to enjoy every moment of his performance.

Film and television acting is much smaller and quieter than that of the Theatre. Nevertheless, with a very few exceptions, the best performers on film and television are actors and actresses from the Theatre, which has taught them their art.

It is the ancient but ever-youthful parent of all entertainment in dramatic form. Much of its work, especially under commercial conditions, may often be trivial and tawdry; but this means that the Theatre should be rescued from such conditions. For in itself, as it has existed on and off for two-and-a-half thousand years, the Theatre is anything but trivial and tawdry. It is the magical place where man meets his image. It is the enduring home of 'dramatic experience', which is surely one of the most searching, rewarding, enchanting of our many different kinds of experience.

Index

Theatres pass on. Theatre, where man meets his image, lives on.

Credits

Alinari 11 (middle), 15 (middle); Bernand 51 (above); Bibliothèque de L'Arsenal (Giraudon) 50 (right); Bibliothèque Nationale 2, 4 (middle), 18 (middle left), 54 (below); B.B.C. 7 (right), 59 (middle), 66; British Museum 6 (left), 18 (above), 25 (middle), 27 (above and middle), 32 (below), 35 (below), 69; Ca Rezzonico (Fiorentini) 32 (above); Ian Chisholm 12-13; Comédie Française (Giraudon) 33 (above and middle), (John Vickers) 50 (below); Commonwealth Relations Office Library 43, 44; Compagnia del Teatro Mediterraneo 15 (right); copyright Elizabeth Dobujinsky 56 (below); Dulwich College Picture Gallery 25 (above); Enthoven Collection (John Vickers) 40 (above); Fiorentini 31 (below); courtesy, Syndics of the Fitzwilliam Museum, Cambridge 58 (middle); Galleria Borghese 17 (above); relief map copyright Geographical Projects Ltd. 10; Goethe-Nationalmuseum, Weimar 41 (above); Governors of the Shakespeare Memorial Theatre 26 (above), 40 (below); Walter Gropius and Architecture Aujourd'hui 60-1; Mrs. M. Holtermann: Albert Bonnier 54 (left); Horniman Museum 7 (left), 9 (left); Don Hunstein 62 (above); I.G.D.A., Novara 42 (below); after painting by Fred Kabotie 6 (right); Landeshauptstadt München Wirtschaftsreferat 39 (above); courtesy James Laver, C.B.E. 34 (above); Lipnitzki 33 (below left), 59 (above); Angus McBean 42 (above left), 59 (below), 63 (below); Mander-Mitchenson Collection 35 (above), 50 (middle), 51 (below); Mansell Collection 34 (below right), 41 (below); Mansell/Alinari 17 (below); Mansell/Anderson 14 (above and below), 16 (above right), 18 (middle right); M.G.M. 67; Museum Antiker Kleinkunst (Hirmer) 11 (above); Musée Condé (Giraudon) 20, 21 (below); Musée du Louvre (Giraudon) 14 (middle), 16 (above); Museo Nazionale 16 (above left); Museo del Prado 22 (below); Musée de Stamboul (Giraudon) 17 (middle); Musée de Versailles (Giraudon) 34 (below left); Nath Black Star 42 (above right); National Gallery, Oslo 54 (right); National Portrait Gallery (John Freeman) 28-9, 36 (above); Piperdrucke Verlags-GmbH, München 48 (above); Presse-Avenir 33 (below right); Michael Relph (John Vickers) 60 (above left); Georg Senftleben 8 (left); Ben Shahn 9 (right); after Gastone Simonetti 21 (above); S.C.R. 56 (above), 57 (below); Edward Steichen: photographed for Vanity Fair 1932 58 (below); Urbino, Ducal Palace (Biffoli) 31 (above); Kalvodova Sis Vanis: 'Chinese Theatre' published by Spring Books 45; Agnes Varda 15 (below left), 63 (below), 65 (below); Vatican Library 18 (below); Vatican Museum 15 (above); John Vickers 3, 26 (below), 55, 57 (above), 62 (below), 65 (below), 68; Victoria and Albert Museum 4 (above), 46 (below); Wadsworth Atheneum 57 (middle); reproduced by permission of the Trustees of the Wallace Collection 5 (middle); photos passim by John Freeman and R. L. Jarmain.